Wings of Silver

The tongue of the just
is as choice silver.
Proverbs 10:20

Wings of Silver

Compiled by Jo Petty

Published by The C. R. Gibson Company

Norwalk, Connecticut

All wise thoughts have been
thought already thousands of times,
but to make them truly ours, we must
think them over again honestly until they
take place in our personal experience.

Contents

The selections in the chapters that
follow have been gathered over a long
period of time. As in our everyday lives
the Bible is the source and basis for
many of our thoughts, so also in this
collection many of the words of wisdom
are choice selections from this precious
volume. In addition there are many
profound thoughts that have come from
the pens of men and women over the years
in different and widely separated parts
of the world. While many of the original
sources are unknown to the compiler,
she nonetheless wishes to acknowledge
the authors, whoever they may be. She has
gathered a collection containing gems
of wisdom, and, although she has brought
nothing of her own, she has supplied
the thread that ties them together.

Love

Love suffers long, and is kind;
Love envies not;
Love vaunts not itself, is not puffed up;
Does not behave itself unseemly,
Seeks not her own,
Is not easily provoked,
Thinks no evil,
Rejoices not in iniquity, but rejoices in the truth;
Bears all things,
Believes all things,
Hopes all things,
Endures all things,
Love never fails!

We dare not violate the law of love any more
than we can defy the law of gravitation.

The test of our love to God
is the love we have one for another.

The language of love is understood by all.

Love ever gives and forgives.

All loves should be stepping stones
to the love of God.

Love is the commandment for fulfilling
all commandments—the rule for fulfilling all rules.

Love works no ill to his neighbor;
therefore, love is the fulfilling of the law.

We love ourselves notwithstanding our faults,
and we ought to love our friends in like manner.

When a friend asks, there is no tomorrow.

If you love, you love others and yourself.
If you hate, you hate others and yourself.

Love never reasons but profusely gives,
gives like a thoughtless prodigal its all,
and trembles then lest it has done too little.

Love knows no limit to its endurance,
no end to its trust, no fading of its hope;
it can outlast anything.
Love still stands when all else has fallen.

Love which has ends will have an end.

We know that all things work together for good
to them that love God.

How shall I do to love? Believe.
How shall I do to believe? Love.

By your love to God, the love to your neighbor
is begotten, and by the love to your neighbor,
your love to God is nourished.

The greatest happiness of life is the conviction
that we are loved, loved for ourselves, or rather
loved in spite of ourselves.

Love is the root of all virtues.

If there is anything better than to be loved,
it is loving.

If we love one another, God dwells in us.

Are you willing to be made willing to forgive?

    If our love were but more simple,
       We should take Him at His word,
    And our lives would be all sunshine
       In the sweetness of the Lord.

He that loves his brother abides in the light.

Hate is sand in the machinery of life—love is oil.

Love is love's reward.

Hatred is like an acid. It can do more damage
to the vessel in which it is stored
than to the object on which it is poured.

God so loved the world that He gave His only
begotten Son, that whosoever believeth in Him
should not perish, but have everlasting life.

The solutions to all our problems
are more of the heart than of the law.

If nobody loves you, be sure it is your own fault.

Love is to the moral nature
what the sun is to the earth.

The husband or wife who harvests thorns should
look to his or her gardening. Either responds to
steadfast love like a plant in the sunshine, sprouting
new dimensions to his or her personality on the side
where the sun shines brightest.

Love, and you shall be loved.

Love understands, and love waits.

Love, like warmth, should beam forth on every side
and bend to every necessity of our brothers.

He prays best who loves best.

Never undervalue any person—the workman loves not
to have his work despised in his presence. Now God is
present everywhere, and every person is His work.

Not where I breathe, but where I love, I live.

Fall in love with yourself and you have no rivals.

Who shall separate us from the love of Christ?
shall tribulation, or distress, or persecution,
or famine, or nakedness, or peril, or sword?

The quarrels of lovers are like summer storms.
Everything is more beautiful when they have passed.

> I hold him great who for love's sake
>   Can give with earnest, generous will.
> But he who takes for love's sweet sake,
>   I think I hold more generous still.

Husbands, love your wives, even as Christ also
loved the Church and gave Himself for it.

Never marry but for love; but see that
you love what is lovely.

> The bravest battle that was ever fought;
>   Shall I tell you where and when?
> On the maps of the world you will find it not;
>   It was fought by the mothers of men.

The remedy for wrongs is to forget them.

> Has some resentment
>   wrought strife and ill-will?
> Love and forgiveness
>   work miracles still.

Be kindly affectioned one to another with
brotherly love; in honor preferring one another.

Be charitable before wealth makes you covetous.

Love your enemies, and do good, and lend,
hoping for nothing again; and your reward shall be great,
and you shall be the children of the Highest:
for He is kind unto the unthankful and to the evil.

Love your enemies, for they tell you your faults.

We must love our fellow man because God
loves him and wills to redeem him.

Whoever in prayer can say 'Our Father'
acknowledges and should feel the brotherhood
of the whole race of mankind.

The spirit of community is our best defense
against communism.

He who despises, despises not men, but God.

You should love your neighbor as yourself,
and you should be good to yourself.

Owe no man anything, but to love one another;
for he that loves another has fulfilled the law.

Science has made the world a neighborhood, but
it will take religion to make it a brotherhood.

Who loves God loves his brother also.

Add to your faith virtue; and to virtue knowledge;
and to knowledge temperance; and to temperance patience;
and to patience godliness; and to godliness
brotherly kindness; and to brotherly kindness LOVE!

To love and be loved is the greatest
happiness of existence.

This is the message that you have heard from the
beginning, that we should love one another.

Being rooted and grounded in love, we are able to
comprehend the breadth, and length, and depth, and
height, and to know the love of Christ, which passes
knowledge, and to be filled with the fulness of God.

Nothing is hardship to love and nothing is hard.

The brightest blaze of intelligence is of less value
than the smallest spark of charity.

Knowledge puffs up, love builds up.

The greatest pleasure of life is love.

Charity gives itself rich; covetousness hoards itself poor.

The injuries we do, and those we suffer,
are seldom weighed in the same balance.

> How empty learning,
>   How vain is art
> But as it mends the life
>   And guides the heart.

There is no instinct like that of the heart.

Set your affection on things above,
and not on things on the earth.

God knows us better than we know ourselves,
and He loves us better, too.

Hate is spiritual suicide.

A child's definition of house and home:
'When you are outside, it looks like a house
but when you are inside, it feels like a home.'

Let us love in deed and in truth
rather than in word and tongue.

Increase and abound in love, one toward another,
and toward all men.

> Only a thought, but the work it wrought,
>   Can never by tongue or pen be taught,
> For it ran through life like a thread of gold
>   And the life bore fruit a hundred fold.

> Only a word! but 'twas spoken in love,
>   With a whispered prayer to the Lord above—
> And the angels in heaven rejoiced once more,
>   For a new-born soul entered through the door.

The word of alms is singular, as if to teach us that
a solitary act of charity scarcely deserves the name.

Where there is room in the heart
there is always room in the house.

Service can be given wherever there are people.

If God so loved us, we ought also to love one another.

A true friend is forever a friend.

Love grows stronger for those who
walk with us day by day.

Love one another.

Love your enemies, do good to those who hate you.

Herein is love, not that we loved God, but
that He loved us and sent His Son
to be the propitiation for our sins.

We pardon as long as we love.

Hatred stirs up strifes; but love covers all sins.

God is love, and he that dwells in love
dwells in God, and God in him.

Love sees what no eye sees;
love hears what no ear hears.

The heart has reasons that reason does not understand.

By this shall all men know that ye are My disciples,
if ye have love one to another.

Many waters cannot quench love,
neither can the floods drown it.

No disguise can long conceal love where it is,
nor feign it where it is not.

All God's laws are God's loves.

A loving heart is the truest wisdom.

Of him that hopes to be forgiven,
it is required that he forgive.

There is no fear in love;
but perfect love casts out fear.

Are we giving the kind of love we seek from God?

> Teach me, Father, when I pray,
>   Not to ask for more,
> But rather let me give my thanks
>   For what is at my door.
> For food and drink, for gentle rain,
>   For sunny skies above,
> For home and friends, for peace and joy,
>   But most of all for love.

Is your love patient and kind? Is it able to
suffer long, to endure every strain placed upon it
in human relations, and still love? Is your love
as steadfast in pointing to God's love as is the
needle of the compass in pointing to the north?
Is your love undiscouraged even by repeated
ingratitude and recurrent failures on the part
of others? Patience and kindness are the fruits of
having Christ live in you. Are you nourishing
your life upon His life by prayer and worship
and studying His word? If so, the fruit of patient
and kind love will grow and will be available
for the healing of other lives.

We cannot give like God, but surely
we may forgive like Him.

To love is to place our happiness
in the happiness of another.

Love not the world,
neither the things that are in the world.
If any man love the world,
the love of the Father is not in him.

There are shadow friendships that appear
only when the sun shines.

Open rebuke is better than secret love.

Joy

Happiness is good.
The place to be happy is here.
The time to be happy is now.
The way to be happy is to help make others happy.

Good cheer is no hindrance to a good life.

The best remedy for discontent
is to count our blessings.

Only the active have the true relish of life.

Sing with gladness,
Banish your sadness.

The gladness of the heart is the life of man,
and the joyfulness of man prolongs his days.

It isn't our position but our disposition
that makes us happy.

No entertainment is so cheap as reading,
nor any pleasure so lasting.

The love of reading enables a man to exchange
the wearisome hours of life, which come
to every one, for hours of delight.

Enjoy present pleasures in such a way as not
to injure future ones.

Scorn a pleasure which gives another pain.

Happiness is neither within us only, or without us;
it is the union of ourselves with God.

He who has not forgiven an enemy has never yet tasted
one of the most sublime enjoyments of life.

Happiness is a running stream, not a stagnant pool.

If pleasure is the highest aim,
it will lead to unhappiness.

If you would know sublime happiness,
sacrifice pleasure for duty.

In diving to the bottom of pleasures
we bring up more gravel than sand.

Blessed are ye, when men revile you, and
persecute you, and shall say all manner of evil against
you falsely, for My sake. Rejoice and be exceedingly
glad; for great is your reward in heaven: for so
persecuted they the prophets which were before you.

Sorrow, like rain, makes roses and mud.

The fear of the Lord makes a merry heart,
and gives joy and gladness, and a long life.

Let those that put their trust in God rejoice:
let them ever shout for joy because God defends them.

Many are on the wrong scent in the pursuit of happiness.

Sing your song and your whole heart
will be in the singing.

Whoso trusts in the Lord, happy is he.

If you don't get everything you want, think of
the things you don't get that you don't want.

Cheerfulness is health;
Melancholy is disease.

The best are not only the happiest, but
the happiest are usually the best.

> A good thing to remember
>   And a better thing to do
> To work with the construction gang
>   And not with the wrecking crew.

My job is never work—the only time
it seems like work is when
I'd rather be doing something else.

The purest pleasures are found in useful work.

To love the All-perfect is happiness.

Cheerfulness is the daughter of employment.

Occupation is the necessary basis of all enjoyment.

Sorrow's best antidote is employment.

Wealth is not his that has it, but his that enjoys it.

The covetous man pines in plenty.

God loves a cheerful giver.

To be without some of the things you want
is an indispensable part of happiness.

What sweet delight a quiet wife affords!

A wife doubles a man's pleasures and divides his cares.

Heaviness in the heart of man makes it stoop:
but a good word makes it glad.

All things are not profitable for all men,
neither has every soul pleasure in everything.

Man should eat and drink and enjoy the good of all
his labor; it is the gift of God.

Happiness or unhappiness depends more
on the way we meet events than on
the nature of those events themselves.

All heaven is interested in the happiness of man.

We cannot be happy unless we think
we are the means of good to others.

The hatred we bear our enemies
injures their happiness less than our own.

Dig a man out of trouble, and the hole which is made
is the grave for your own sorrows.

Not just live and let live,
but live and help live.

Happy is the man that findeth wisdom,
and the man that getteth understanding:
For the merchandise of it is better than
the merchandise of silver, and the gain
thereof than fine gold.
She is more precious than rubies: and
all the things thou canst desire are not to
be compared unto her.
Length of days is in her right hand; and
in her left hand riches and honor.
Her ways are ways of pleasantness, and
all her paths are peace.
She is a tree of life to them that lay
hold upon her: and happy is every one that
retaineth her.

They that sow in tears shall reap in joy.

There are no riches above a sound body,
and no joy above the joy of the heart.

Love your own soul, and comfort your heart,
remove sorrow from you: for sorrow has killed many,
and there is not profit therein.

Weeping may endure for a night,
but joy comes in the morning.

A merry heart does good like a medicine:
but a broken spirit dries the bones.

Pleasant words are as a honeycomb,
sweet to the soul, and health to the bones.

Health makes you feel now is the best time of the year.

Unhappiness is not knowing what we want
and killing ourselves to get it.

Some pleasures are more trouble than trouble.

Happiness is enhanced by others
but does not depend upon others.

He enjoys much who is thankful for little.

Joy on account of
or joy in spite of?

The happiest person is the person who
thinks the most interesting thoughts,
and we grow happier as we grow older.

O satisfy us early with Thy mercy;
that we may rejoice and be glad all our days.

Happiness is not a reward—it is a consequence.

When you have thanked the Lord
for every blessing sent, but little time
will then remain for murmur or lament.

Your joy no man takes from you.

The joy of the Lord is your strength.

In the world you shall have tribulation,
but be of good cheer.

He that is of a merry heart has a continual feast.

Live joyfully with the wife whom thou lovest
all the days of the life of thy vanity . . .
for that is thy portion in this life,
and in thy labor . . . under the sun.

To be happy at home is the
ultimate aim of all ambition.

He is happiest who finds his peace in his home.

A man travels the world over in search of
what he needs and returns home to find it.

Activity and sadness are incompatible.

All people smile in the same language.

A smile is a curve that can set a lot of things straight.

A life of pleasure can be the most sorrowful life.

The flower that follows the sun
does so even in cloudy days.

O for the good old days when I was so unhappy.

A sorrow shared is a sorrow halved.

Remember there are no bad days—
some are just better than others.

The supreme pleasure is to promote the joy of others.

A child of God should be a visible beatitude
of joy and happiness and a living doxology
for gratitude and adoration.

It is good to let a little sunshine out as well as in.

There is no cosmetic for beauty like happiness.

Don't spend your days stringing and tuning your
instrument—start making music now.

A link of man's mind may be forged
by the heart of a song.

A humorist is a man who feels bad
but feels good about it.

How tasteless are the passing pleasures of this world!

Happy is that people whose God is the Lord.

A merry heart makes a cheerful countenance.

He that loves wisdom loves life;
and they that seek her early shall be filled with joy.

Count it all joy when you fall into sundry
temptations, for the trial of your faith
brings forth patience.

If ignorance is bliss, why aren't more people
jumping up and down for joy?

The principal business of life is to enjoy it.

Do not put off until tomorrow
what can be enjoyed today.

Be glad in the Lord, and rejoice, ye righteous:
and shout for joy, all ye that are upright in heart.

O Happy Day that fixed my choice
on Thee my Savior and my God.
Well may this glowing heart rejoice
and tell its rapture all abroad.

Rejoice in the Lord alway and again I say, rejoice.

The spirit of melancholy would often take its flight
from us if only we would take up the song of praise.

Joy is everywhere.

Happiness is never caused by circumstances alone.

I am not fully dressed until I adorn myself
with a smile of joy.

We may be sure we are not pleasing God
if we are not happy ourselves.

The Lord has done great things for us:
whereof we are glad.

No thoroughly occupied man
was ever yet very miserable.

Labor, if it were not necessary for the existence,
would be indispensable for the happiness of men.

The busy have no time for tears.

Business before pleasure and neither before God.

Nothing is pleasure that is not spiced with variety.

I do not believe in doing for pleasure
things I do not like to do.

Religion may not keep you from sinning
but it takes the joy out of it.

Joy shall be in heaven over one sinner that repenteth,
more than over ninety and nine just persons
which need no repentance.

O for a thanksgiving for every heart beat
and a song for every breath.

The good things of life are not to be had singly,
but come to us with a mixture; like a schoolboy's
holiday, with a task affixed to the tail of it.

Life would be tolerably agreeable
if it were not for its amusements.

The fruit derived from labor
is the sweetest of pleasures.

I shall not be gloomy as long as the sun shines.

A man of meditation is happy, not for an hour,
or a day, but quite round the circle of his years.

The foolish man seeks happiness in the distance;
the wise man grows it under his feet.

A cheerful friend is like a sunny day.

Smile for the joy of others.

Delight yourself in the Lord;
and He shall give you the desires of your heart.

The prayer of the upright is God's delight.

Peace

The Lord is my shepherd;
  I shall not want.
He maketh me to lie down in green pastures:
  He leadeth me beside the still waters.
He restoreth my soul:
He leadeth me in the paths of righteousness
  for His name's sake.
Yea, though I walk through the valley
  of the shadow of death,
I will fear no evil: for Thou art with me;
  Thy rod and Thy staff they comfort me.
Thou preparest a table before me
  in the presence of mine enemies:
Thou anointest my head with oil;
  My cup runneth over.
Surely goodness and mercy shall follow me
  all the days of my life:
And I will dwell in the house
  of the Lord forever.

Be strong and of good courage; be not afraid,
neither be dismayed: for the Lord your God
is with you wherever you go.

Is your soul running as though being pursued,
with no opportunity to rest and feed?

He that loves silver shall not be satisfied with
silver; nor he that loves abundance with increase.

Rest is the sweet sauce of labor.

Watching for riches consumes the flesh,
and the care thereof drives away sleep.

Watching care will not let a man slumber,
as a sore disease breaks sleep.

When you have accomplished your daily task,
go to sleep in peace; God is awake!

I will lay me down in peace and sleep:
for Thou, Lord, only makes me dwell in safety.

If I am at war with myself,
I can bring little peace to my fellow man.

I have learned in whatsoever state I am,
therewith to be content.

All men desire peace; few desire
the things which make for peace.

Peace is the happy, natural state of man.

As long as man stands in his own way,
everything seems to be in his way.

A good memory is fine—but the ability to forget
is the true test of greatness.

Well-arranged time is the surest mark
of a well-arranged mind.

I am easy to please but difficult to satisfy.

The thing to put aside for one's old age
is all thought of retirement.

Doing nothing is the most tiresome job in the world
because you cannot quit and rest.

The sleep of a laboring man is sweet,
whether he eat little or much;
but the abundance of the rich
will not suffer him to sleep.

I was angry with my friend:
I told my wrath, my wrath did end.
I was angry with my foe;
I hid my wrath, my wrath did grow.

A man's venom poisons himself more than his victim.

Marriage with a good woman
is a harbor in the tempest of life;
with a bad woman, it is a tempest in the harbor.

Few things are more bitter than to feel bitter.

The evening of a well-spent life
brings its lamp with it.

Work is not the cause—
Rest is not the cure.

Rest not from duty, but find rest in it.

Better is a handful with quietness, than both
the hands full with travail and vexation of spirit.

Consider wherein you agree with your opponent
rather than wherein you differ.

I'm so accustomed to being tense
that when I'm calm I get nervous.

How good and how pleasant it is for brothers
to dwell together in unity.

The Lord is on my side; I will not fear:
what can man do unto me?

Be careful for nothing; but in everything
by prayer and supplication with thanksgiving
let your requests be made known unto God.
And the peace of God, which passes all understanding
shall keep your hearts and minds through Christ Jesus.

To be carnally minded is death;
but to be spiritually minded is life and peace.

Think little of what others think of you.

Don't hurry, don't worry,
Do your best, and leave the rest.

If we find not repose in ourselves,
it is in vain to seek it elsewhere.

Fear nothing so much as sin.

There is no witness so terrible—no accuser
so powerful—as conscience which dwells within us.

There is no peace, says the Lord, unto the wicked.

If it be possible, as much as lies in you,
live peaceably with all men.

Mark the perfect man and behold the upright;
for the end of that man is peace.

Worry—a mental tornado—a dog chasing its own tail.

To carry care to bed
is to sleep with a pack on your back.

The secret of contentment
is knowing how to enjoy what you have.

This is maturity:
To be able to stick with a job until it is finished;
to be able to bear an injustice without wanting to get even;
to be able to carry money without spending it;
and to do one's duty without being supervised.

Godliness with contentment is great gain.

Religion has long been used to comfort the troubled.
May it sometime be used to trouble the comfortable.

Pure gold can lie for a month in the furnace
without losing a grain.

The peace within becomes the harmony without.

Jesus said: 'Come unto Me, all ye that labor
and are heavy laden, and I will give you rest.'

God is not the author of confusion, but of peace.

Follow after the things which make for peace,
and things wherewith one may edify another.

Being justified by faith, we have
peace with God through our Lord Jesus Christ.

I shall grow old, but never lose life's zest
Because the road's last turn will be the best.
   Expect the best!

It lies not in the past.
God ever keeps the good wine till the last.
Beyond are nobler work and sweeter rest.
   Expect the best!

The Lord is my light and my salvation;
whom shall I fear?
The Lord is the strength of my life;
of whom shall I be afraid?

In solitude we are least alone.

I should know myself better
if there were not so many of me.

Mercy and truth are met together;
righteousness and peace have kissed each other.

My son, forget not My law;
but let your heart keep My commandments:
for length of days, and long life,
and peace shall they add to you.

How men treat us will make little difference
when we know we have God's approval.

One who is afraid of lying
is usually afraid of nothing else.

Be still and know that I am God.

Cast all your care upon God; for He cares for you.

He that dwells in the secret place of the most High
shall abide under the shadow of the Almighty.
I will say of the Lord, He is my refuge and my fortress:
my God, in Him will I trust.
Surely He shall deliver you from the snare of the fowler,
and from the noisome pestilence.
He shall cover you with His feathers,
and under His wings shall you trust:
His truth shall be your shield and buckler.
You shall not be afraid for the terror of night:
nor for the arrow that flies by day.

Long suffering

Great victories come, not through ease but by
fighting valiantly and meeting hardships bravely.

If you can't have the best of everything,
make the best of everything you have.

Patience is the finest and worthiest part of fortitude.

We can do anything we want to
if we stick to it long enough.

If you faint in the day of adversity,
your strength is small.

The secret of success is constancy to purpose.

Men do not fail; they give up trying.

The grinding that would wear away
to nothing a lesser stone, merely
serves to give luster to a diamond.

Sometimes a noble failure serves the world
as faithfully as a distinguished success.

Difficulties strengthen the mind,
as labor does the body.

The man who rows the boat
doesn't have time to rock it.

Luck means the hardships and privations which
you have not hesitated to endure, the long
nights you have devoted to work. Luck means
the appointments you have never failed to keep;
the trains you have never failed to catch.

> A little more determination,
>   A little more pluck,
> A little more work—
>   that's LUCK.

Mastery in any art comes only with long practice.

If at first you do succeed, try something harder.

A fella doesn't last long on what he has done;
he has to keep delivering!

Free enterprise gives everybody
a chance to get to the top. Some
depend too much on the free
and not enough on the enterprise.

The early bird gets the firm.

Not every one that says unto Me, Lord,
Lord, shall enter into the kingdom of heaven;
but he that does the will of My Father which is in heaven.

As sure as ever God puts his children in the furnace,
He will be in the furnace with them.

It is not until we have passed through the furnace
that we are made to know how much dross
there is in our composition.

I have fought a good fight, I have finished
my course, I have kept the Faith; henceforth
there is laid up for me a crown of righteousness, which the Lord, the righteous Judge,
shall give me at that day: and not to me only,
but unto all them also that love His appearing.

The grass is greener on the other side,
but it is just as hard to mow.

A smooth sea never made a skillful mariner.

The cloud that darkens the present hour
may brighten all our future days.

It is easier to fight for one's principles
than to live up to them.

Life, misfortune, isolation, abandonment, poverty
are battlefields, which have their heroes,—
heroes obscure, but sometimes greater
than those who become illustrious.

Salvation is free but being Christian is costly.

Shoot at everything and hit nothing.

Making excuses doesn't change the truth.

Could not the victories of the weaker be the greater?

Give wind and tide a chance to change.

The error of youth is to believe that intelligence
is a substitute for experience,
while the error of age is to believe
that experience is a substitute for intelligence.

Judge nothing before the time.

Don't lessen the lesson.

Experience is what makes you wonder how
it got a reputation for being the best teacher.

Cast out the beam first of your own eye;
and then you shall see clearly
to cast out the mote of your brother's eye.

If I could only see the road you came,
With all the jagged rocks and crooked ways,
I might more kindly think of your misstep
And only praise.

It is difficult to say who does us the most mischief—
our enemies with the worst intentions
or our friends with the best.

Many are the afflictions of the righteous;
but the Lord delivers him out of them all.

If I could only know the heartaches you have felt,
The longing for the things that never came,
I would not misconstrue your erring then
Nor ever blame.

All people are born equal. Each has a right to earn
his niche by the sweat of his brow.
But some sweat more and carve larger niches.

Remember there's blue sky behind the blackest cloud.

When you begin to coast
you know you're on the downgrade.

You that fear the Lord, wait for His mercy;
and go not aside, lest you fall.

If your cup seems too bitter, if your
burden seems too heavy, be sure
that it is the wounded hand that is
holding the cup, and that it is
He who carries the cross that is
carrying the burden.

God will not look you over for medals,
degrees, or diplomas, but for scars.

Our light affliction, which is but for a moment,
works for us a far more exceeding
and eternal weight of glory.

The sufferings of this present time
are not worthy to be compared
with the glory which shall be revealed in us.

The dictionary is the only place
success comes before work.

Set your heart aright, constantly endure,
and make not haste in time of trouble.

It is better to wear out than to rust out.

Trouble and perplexity drive me to prayer,
and prayer drives away perplexity and trouble.

Better limp all the way to heaven
than not get there at all.

Sanctified afflictions are spiritual promotions.

He surely is most in need of another's patience,
who has none of his own.

They also serve who only stand and wait.

Wait on the Lord: be of good courage,
and He shall strengthen your heart:
wait, I say, on the Lord.

They that wait upon the Lord
shall renew their strength;
they shall mount up with wings as eagles;
they shall run, and not be weary;
and they shall walk, and not faint.

Parents who wish to train their children
in the way they should go, must go in the way
which they would have their children go.

The most generous vine, if not pruned,
runs out into many superfluous stems
and grows at last weak and fruitless;
so does the best man if he be not cut short
in his desires and pruned with afflictions.

In youth we run into difficulties;
in age difficulties run into us.

Young men these days seem to
confuse starting at the bottom
with getting in on the ground floor.

God sometimes washes the eyes of His children
with tears that they may read aright
His providence and His commandments.

Sometime, when all life's lessons have been learned, . . .
we shall see how all God's plans were right,
and how what seemed reproof was love most true.

Patience is not passive; on the contrary
it is active; it is concentrated strength.

Make haste slowly.

Anytime a man takes a stand,
there'll come a time when he'll be tested
to see how firm his feet are planted.

You and I cannot determine what other men
shall think and say about us.
We can only determine what they ought
to think of us and say about us.

You can tell some people aren't afraid
of work by the way they fight it.

Toil awhile, endure awhile, believe always,
and never turn back.

Be not weary in well doing.

It does one good to be somewhat parched by the heat
and drenched by the rain of life.

Adversity is the only balance to weigh friends —
prosperity is no just scale.

God will not suffer you to be tempted
above that you are able; but will
with the temptation also make a way to escape,
that ye may be able to bear it.

Christianity has not been tried and found wanting;
it has been found difficult and not tried.

Fundamentally true ideas possess greater
ultimate power than physical might.

You can't slide uphill.

Men are apt to settle a question rightly
when it is discussed freely.

People do not lack strength; they lack will.

The quitter never wins.
The winner never quits.

> Be no more by a storm dismayed,
>   For by it the full-grown seeds are laid;
> And though the tree by its might it shatters,
>   What then, if thousands of seeds it scatters?

Life is never so bad at its worst
that it is impossible to live;
it is never so good at its best
that it is easy to live.

Borrowing trouble from the future
does not deplete the supply.

Living the good life is not a fair weather job.

Make the most of the best and the least of the worst.

Troubles are often the tools
by which God fashions us for better things.

Never despair, but if you do, work on in despair.

In great attempts it is glorious even to fail.

It is by those who have suffered that
the world is most advanced.

If we were faultless we should not be
so much annoyed by the defects of others.

Speakers have been showering us with
pearls of wisdom for centuries, and
if their valuable advice were laid end to end,
it would still be just as good as new.
Very little of it has ever been used.

If you are not able to make yourself what you wish,
how can you expect to mold another to your will?

The way of the world is to praise dead saints
and persecute living ones.

Temperament is temper that is too old to spank.

Building boys is easier than mending men.

To find fault is easy; to do better may be difficult.

It is the practice of the multitude
to bark at eminent men as little dogs at strangers.

Understanding is the secret of withstanding.

If a man empties his purse into his head,
no man can take it from him.

No one agrees with the opinions of others.
He merely agrees with his own opinions
expressed by somebody else.

An obstinate man does not hold opinions —
they hold him.

He that has no cross will have no crown.

The greatest affliction of life
is never to be afflicted.

Carry your cross patiently and with perfect
submission, and in the end it shall carry you.

A just man falls seven times, and rises up again.

What man calls fortune is from God.

A purpose is the eternal condition of success.

Though our outward man perish,
yet the inward man is renewed day by day.

Fret not thyself because of evil men,
neither be envious at the wicked;
for there shall be no reward to the evil man;
the candle of the wicked shall be put out.

That which is painful to the body
may be profitable to the soul.

Good timber does not grow in ease,
The stronger wind, the stronger trees;
The farther sky the greater length,
The more the storms the more the strength.
By sun and cold, by rain and snow,
In tree or man good timber grows.

Patience is bitter, but its fruit is sweet.

The aim of education is to teach us
how to think, not what to think.

Instruction may end in the schoolroom,
but education ends only with life.

There are those who are ever learning and never
able to come to the knowledge of the truth.

A college graduate is a person who had
a chance to get an education.

Talent knows what to do;
tact knows when and how to do it.

Poise is the art of raising the eyebrows
instead of the roof.

Character development is the true aim of education.

An ounce of pluck is worth a ton of luck.

The same furnace that liquifies the gold
hardens the clay.

The worst men often give the best advice.

Nothing is done finally and right.
Nothing is known positively and completely.

The late blooming virtues can be the very best.

Confront improper conduct,
not by retaliation, but by example.

Firmness is that admirable quality in ourselves
that is merely stubbornness in others.

Whosoever will save his life shall lose it:
and whosoever shall lose his life
for My sake shall find it.

It is easier to be critical than correct.

The secret of success is hard work.

He conquers who endures.

Let those who suffer according to the will of God
commit the keeping of their souls to Him in well doing,
as unto a faithful Creator.

As threshing separates the wheat from the chaff,
so does affliction purify virtue.

Be not overcome of evil, but overcome evil with good.

Idleness is the burial of a living person.

Recreation is not being idle; it is
easing the wearied part by change of occupation.

The clock of life is wound but once,
And no man has the power to tell
Just when the hands will stop
At late or early hour.
Now is the only time you own:
Live, love, toil with a will,
Place no faith in tomorrow;
For the clock may then be still.

The virtue lies in the struggle, not in the prize.

Gentleness

We cannot always oblige,
but we can always speak obligingly.

Wouldn't it be nice if we could find other things
as easily as we find fault?

A word of kindness is seldom spoken in vain,
while witty sayings are easily lost
as the pearls slipping from a broken string.

No man has it so good but that two or three words
can dishearten, and there is no calamity
but a few right words can hearten.

Speak not evil one of another.

To listen well is as to talk well
and is as essential to all true conversation.

Speak gently — it is better far
to rule by love than fear.
Speak gently — let no harsh words
mar the good we might do here.

Diplomacy is to do and say
the nastiest thing in the nicest way.

Let the words of my mouth and the meditation
of my heart be always acceptable in Thy sight,
O Lord, my strength and my Redeemer.

The greatest truths are the simplest;
and so are the greatest men.

A small unkindness is a great offense.

> I have wept in the night for the shortness of sight
> That to somebody's need made me blind;
> But I never have yet felt a twinge of regret
> For being a little too kind.

As we have opportunity, let us do good unto all men.

Be careful how you live; you may be
the only Bible some people read.

The servant of the Lord must not strive,
but be gentle unto all men, apt to teach, patient,
in meekness instructing those who oppose themselves.

The milk of human kindness never curdles.

Man's inhumanity to man makes
countless thousands mourn.

Be kind, one to another, tenderhearted, forgiving
one another, even as God for Christ's
sake has forgiven you.

Good manners are the small coin of virtue.

He who reforms himself has done much
toward reforming others.

Bless them which persecute you.

Rejoice with them that do rejoice
and weep with them that weep.

Be not forgetful to entertain strangers:
for thereby some have entertained angels unawares.

Today's profits are yesterday's goodwill ripened.

A good name is rather to be chosen than great riches,
and loving favor rather than silver and gold.

To belittle is to be little.

Let me grow lovely, growing old —
So many fine things do:
Lace and ivory and gold
And silks need not be new.
There is healing in old trees,
Old streets a glamor hold.
Why may not I, as well as these,
Grow lovely, growing old?

One who grimly declares, 'I shall do my duty,'
is facing a drab experience. A smile and kindly
understanding can generate warmth
to melt the grimness and compulsion.

A noble heart, like the sun shows its greatest
countenance in its lowest estate.

The wisdom that is from above is first pure,
then peaceable, gentle, and easy to be entreated,
full of mercy and good fruits,
without partiality, and without hypocrisy.

What we need is not new light, but new sight;
not new paths, but new strength to walk in the
old ones; not new duties but new strength from
on High to fulfill those that are plain before us.

Punctuality is the politeness of kings
and the duty of gentle people everywhere.

True politeness is perfect ease and freedom;
it simply consists in treating others
just as you love to be treated yourself.

It is they who do their duties in every-day and
trivial matters who fulfill them on great occasions.

It is only imperfection that is intolerant
of what is imperfect. The more perfect we
are, the more gentle and quiet we become
toward the defects of others.

It isn't so much what's on the table that matters
but what's on the chairs.

Be of the same mind one toward another. Mind not
high things but condescend to men of low estate.

A rolling stone gathers no moss
but it obtains a certain polish.

Culture is one thing and varnish another.

The habit of expressing appreciation
is oil on troubled waters. It is the essence of
graciousness, kindness, and fair dealing.
Fortunately, it is a habit that can be formed
by anyone who will take the trouble.

What you dislike in another,
take care to correct in yourself.

Manners are minor morals.

> A little more tired at the close of the day,
>   A little less anxious to have our way,
> A little less anxious to scold and blame,
>   A little more care for a brother's name;
> And so we are nearing the journey's end,
>   Where time and eternity meet and blend.

A soft answer turns away wrath,
but grievous words stir up anger.

A real friend is one who helps us
to think our noblest thoughts, put forth our
best efforts, and to be our best selves.

Goodness

For kindness is indeed sublime and worth the
trouble anytime. Sincerity is all we need to help us
do a friendly deed.

Give to him that asks you;
from him that would borrow of you turn not away.

As you would that men should do to you,
do you also to them likewise.

Be great in act, as you have been in thought. Suit
the action to the word and the word to the action.

No man can be good to others
without being good to himself.

Our deeds determine us as much
as we determine our deeds.

The rung of a ladder was never meant to rest upon,
but only to hold a man's foot long enough to
enable him to put the other one higher.

Judge not, and you shall not be judged:
condemn not, and you shall not be condemned:
forgive, and you shall be forgiven.

Jesus went about doing good.

Whatever makes good Christians
makes them good citizens.

The hand that's dirty with honest labor
is fit to shake with any neighbor.

To him that knows to do good, and does it not,
to him it is sin.

Can my creed be recognized in my deed?

The goodness of God endures continually.

The good-natured person is described in one
of Paul's letters — 'envieth not — not puffed up —
not easily provoked — seeketh no evil.'
To sum it up, his nature is GOOD.

Be not weary in well doing; for in due season
you shall reap, if you faint not.

Good depends not on things but on the use
we make of things.

He who masters his words will master his works.

Not the hearers of the law are just before God,
but the doers of the law shall be justified.

Man looks on the outward appearance;
but God looks on the heart.

Sin is not in things but in the wrong use of things.

The man who is mean is meaner to himself
than anyone else.

Abhor that which is evil;
cleave to that which is good.

We persuade others by being in earnest ourselves.

Be what you say and say what you are.

Let word, creed, and deed be integrated in one truth.

Honesty is always the best policy.

A problem honestly stated is half solved.

No man has good enough memory
to make a successful liar.

Truth cannot be killed with the sword
nor abolished by law.

It is better to suffer for speaking the truth than
that the truth should suffer for want of speaking it.

Truth is not only violated by falsehood;
it may be equally outraged by silence.

It is easy to tell a lie; but hard
to tell only one lie.

If we ever have a golden age, it will be because
golden hearts are beating in it.

Character is a diamond that scratches
every other stone.

There is no liberty in wrong-doing.

It is difficult to believe in the goodness
of disagreeable people.

God listens to our hearts rather than to our lips.

Better is a little with righteousness than
great revenues without right.

Money dishonestly acquired is never worth
its cost, while a good conscience never costs
as much as it is worth.

Prefer loss before unjust gain.

O, what a tangled web we weave, when first
we practice to deceive.

Discover what is true and practice what is good.

No service is too small and none too great,
from the giving of a cup of cold water to
the laying down of one's life.

Many faults in our neighbor should be of
less consequence to us than one of the
smallest in ourselves.

The best way to succeed in life is to act
on the advice you give to others.

If you follow righteousness, you shall obtain her
and put her on as a glorious long robe.

No man has a right to do as he pleases,
except when he pleases to do right.

Nothing can be truly great which is not right.

Everything great is not always good, but all
good things are great.

When we snub, we snub Christ;
When we neglect, we neglect Christ;
When we hate, we hate Christ.
Wherever we turn, there is Christ in one
of our brothers to bless or to hurt.

He that abides in Me, and I in him,
the same brings forth much fruit:
for without Me you can do nothing.

He that does good for good's sake
seeks neither praise nor reward,
but he is sure of both in the end.

Life is a steep grade, and we should welcome
every opportunity to give our friends a lift
when they need it.

There may be times when you cannot find help,
but there is no time when you cannot give help.

Do good with what you have, or it will do you no good.

If you do what you should not, you must bear
what you would not.

We reform others unconsciously when we walk uprightly.

Prove all things; hold fast that which is good.

Act as if each day were given you for Christmas,
just as eager, just as proud!

Help your brother's boat across, and lo!
your own has reached the shore.

He is greatest who is most useful to others.

Whatever is worth doing at all, is worth doing well.

Good thoughts are little better than good dreams
except they be put in action.

Practice an attitude of gratitude.

What you are thunders so loud
I cannot hear what you say.

The man who lives by himself and for himself
is apt to be corrupted by the company he keeps.

He who is not liberal with what he has
deceives himself when he thinks he would
be liberal if he had more.

Whatsoever a man sows, that shall he also reap.

He who wishes to secure the good of others
has already secured his own.

There is so much good in the worst of us, and so
much bad in the best of us, that it behooves
all of us not to talk about the rest of us.

    Be the labor great or small
    Do it well or not at all.

If the cake is bad, what good is the frosting?

The greatest of faults is to be conscious of none.

At doing what we shouldn't we are all experts!

From the errors of others a wise man
corrects his own.

To err is human; to forgive divine.

Legal immunity does not confer moral immunity.

Recompense to no man evil for evil.

The prodigal robs his heir; the miser robs himself.

To be good is fine, but to be proud of it
ruins the whole thing.

Whosoever shall compel you to go a mile,
go with him two.

Whosoever shall smite you on your right cheek,
turn to him the other also.

A good man leaves a good legacy if he leaves his children educated.

The naked truth is not indecent.

The study of God's word, for the purpose of discovering God's will, is the secret discipline which has formed the greatest characters.

Whatsoever things are true,
Whatsoever things are honest,
Whatsoever things are just,
Whatsoever things are pure,
Whatsoever things are lovely,
Whatsoever things are of good report,
If there be any virtue,
If there be any praise,
Think on these things.

Faith

Faith is the substance of things hoped for,
the evidence of things not seen.

I know not what the future holds, but I know
Who holds the future.

Some men have many reasons why they cannot
do what they want, when all they need
is one reason why they can.

The trial of your faith is more precious than gold.

Earnestly contend for the faith which was
once delivered to the saints.

The blind with their hand in God's,
can see more clearly than those
who can see who have no faith.

Never put a question mark where God puts a period.

Faith is the awareness of utter
helplessness without God.

Know this that the trying of your faith works
patience. Let patience have her perfect work,
that you may be perfect and entire, wanting nothing.

Use your gifts faithfully, and they shall be
enlarged; practice what you know, and you shall
attain to higher knowledge.

Have faith in the force of right
and not the right of force.

Only you can do it, but you can't do it alone.

The word disappointment is not
in the Dictionary of Faith.

All unbelief is the belief of a lie.

Sometimes faith must learn a deeper rest,
And trust God's silence when He does not speak.

Faith grows in the valley.

Faith and works are twins.

Faith is the victory that overcomes the world.

The well of Providence is deep.
It's the buckets we bring to it that are small.

Any trouble that is too small to take to God
in prayer is too small to worry about.

Take one step toward God, and He will take
two steps toward you.

Faith does not exclude work,
but only the merit of work.

The end of our faith is the salvation of our souls.

Christianity regulates the whole man in all
departments of his existence.

God is only a prayer away.

Our grand business in life is not to see
what lies dimly at a distance,
but to do what lies clearly at hand.

The horizon is not the boundary of the world.

The things which are seen are temporal,
but the things which are not seen are eternal.

He that believes on the Son has everlasting life.

Be persuaded that, what He has promised,
He is able also to perform.

> All efforts to destroy are vain —
> God's Holy Word will still remain;
> So hammer on, ye hostile hands,
> Your hammers break, God's anvil stands.

Prayer is the key in the hand of faith
which unlocks heaven's storehouse.

Men do not need to be instructed how to
pray in the midst of battle.

Except the Lord build the house, they labor in
vain that build it; except the Lord keep the city,
the watchman wakes but in vain.

A man is not justified by the works of the law,
but by the faith of Jesus Christ.

Even if you knew how much time I spend on my knees
you do not know how much I pray.

God cares not for much prayers but good prayers.

Reach out the hand of faith and touch
the throttle of prayer.

The prayer of faith shall save the sick,
and the Lord shall raise him up.

> Should Thy mercy send me sorrow, toil, and woe,
> Or should pain attend me on my path below;
> Grant that I may never fail Thy hand to see;
> Grant that I may ever cast my care on Thee.

By grace are you saved through faith;
and that not of yourselves: it is the gift of God —
not of works lest any man should boast.

The Bible is a surer and safer guide through life
than human reason.

Faith does not spring out of feeling
but feeling out of faith.
The less we feel the more we should trust.

No cloud can overshadow a true Christian,
but his faith will discern a rainbow on it.

The real victory of Faith
is to trust God in the dark.

If a man could have his wishes,
he would double his troubles.

If you have faith as a grain of mustard seed,
nothing shall be impossible unto you.

Ask in faith, nothing wavering.
For he that wavers is like a wave of the sea
driven with the wind and tossed.

Trust in the Lord, and do good; so shall you
dwell in the land, and verily you shall be fed.

Youth and Age look upon life from the opposite ends
of the telescope; to the one it is exceedingly long,
to the other exceedingly short.

It is impossible that anything so natural,
so necessary, and so universal as death should
ever have been designed as an evil to mankind.

> Teach me to live that I may dread
> the grave as little as my bed.

Draw near to God, and He will draw near to you.

God did not remove the Red Sea, and He will lead us
through our difficulties if they cannot be removed.

We walk by faith, not by sight.

Whatever He sends, whether sunshine or dew,
is needed for your soul's health.

Take no thought for your life, what you shall eat;
neither for your body, what you shall put on.
The life is more than meat, and the body
is more than raiment.

The Bible is a mirror in which man
sees himself as he is.

Faith comes by hearing,
and hearing by the word of God.

Faith takes God at His word whatever He says.

Consider the lilies of the field, how they grow;
they toil not, neither do they spin,
yet I say unto you that Solomon in all his
glory was not arrayed like one of these.

All else fail — Thou dost not fail!
I rest upon Thy word alone.

I am the bread of life: he that comes to Me
shall never hunger; and he that believes on Me
shall never thirst.

I can do all things through Christ
Who strengthens me.

Our strength lies in our dependence upon God.

Works is faith made perfect.

He gives the very best to those
who leave the choice with Him.

The test of our faith is our eagerness
to proclaim the good news.

I am the way, the truth, and the life:
No man comes unto the Father, but by Me.

>   You are coming to the King —
>   Large petitions with you bring —
>   For His grace and power are such —
>   None can ever ask too much.

The sheep in the Shepherd's arm looks only
into the face of the Shepherd and not to the
wolves nearby seeking to harm him.

Trust in the Lord with all your heart;
and lean not unto your own understanding.

Examine yourselves, whether you be in the faith;
prove your own selves.

No one is safe who does not learn
to trust God for every thing.

You have not, because you ask not.

Stagger not at the promise of God
through unbelief; but be strong in faith,
giving glory to God.

A ship is safest in deep water.

Fear God, and we shall have no need to fear
Adam or the *atom*.

> You turn to God when storm clouds brew,
>   And pray to Him for light;
> Would you know all God's good for you,
>   Try praying when the skies are bright.

Never think that God's delays are God's denials.

True prayer always receives what is asked
or something better.

Faith is the eyesight of the soul.

Here, believe.
There, understand.

Nothing is or can be accidental with God.

God will supply, but we must apply.

With God all things are possible.

The effectual, fervent prayer of
a righteous man avails much.

There are moments when whatever be the attitude
of the body, the soul is on its knees.

God is able to do exceeding
abundantly above all that we ask or think,
according to the power that works in us.

The law of prayer is more powerful and just
as universal as the law of gravity.

Our prayer is the sum of our duty.
Ask God for what we need and watch
and labor for all that we ask.

Whatever we beg of God, let us also work for it.

Pray our work and work our prayers.

By trials, God is shaping us for higher things.
We are always in the forge or on the anvil.

If God be for us, who can be against us?

How calmly may we commend ourselves
to the hands of Him Who bears up the world.

Continue in prayer, and watch in the
same with thanksgiving.

O Lord, open Thou my lips and my mouth
shall show forth Thy praise.

Are we loaded down with an inadequate religion
rather than being lifted up with a faith
which really sustains?

A weak man becomes powerful when he is in
contact with the mighty force of God.

The gospel of Christ is the power of God
unto salvation to every one that believes.

Believe in God, and He will help you;
order your way aright, and trust in Him.

The things which are impossible with men
are possible with God.

The just shall live by faith.

Launch out into the deep — let the shoreline go.

The outlook may be dark,
but the uplook is glorious.

Meekness

Humble yourselves in the sight of the Lord,
and He shall lift you up.

Not many of us are material for greatness,
according to the general acceptance of the term,
but each has something to give to justify
the gift of life. The humblest can become
kindly and easy to live with.

The meek will He guide in judgment:
and the meek will He teach His way.

True greatness consists in being
great in little things.

What one is in little things he is also in great.

A small leak will sink a great ship.

It is easy to dodge an elephant but not a fly.

God has two dwellings: one in heaven and
the other in a meek and thankful heart.

A modest man ever shuns making himself
the subject of his conversation.

Pride makes us esteem ourselves;
vanity desires the esteem of others.

Give many men your ear but few your voice.

Though the Lord be high;
yet has He respect unto the lowly.

Be subject one to another, and be clothed
with humility; for God resists the proud
and gives grace to the humble.

Be sure of this: you are dreadfully like other people.

The greater we are, the more humble we are.

Think not of yourself more highly
than you ought to think.

May I remember that mankind got along very well
before my birth and in all probability
will get along very well after my death.

Whosoever shall exalt himself shall be abased;
and he that shall humble himself shall be exalted.

A good penny is better than a bad nickel.

Humility is only gratitude.

To accept good advice is but to increase
one's own ability

Humility is the solid foundation of all the virtues.

He who glories, let him glory in the Lord.

He that is warned by the folly of others
has perhaps attained the soundest wisdom.

Knowledge makes men humble, and true
genius is ever modest.

Be not like the cock who thought
the sun rose to hear him crow.

We may learn silence from the talkative,
toleration from the intolerant,
kindness from the unkind.

Speak as to be only the arrow in the bow
which the Almighty draws.

No person can ever be a complete failure,
for he may serve as a horrible example.

The man who leaves home to set the world on fire
often comes back for more matches.

May we all be praying publicans lest we should
become self-righteous Pharisees.

Self satisfaction dulls the ambition and blunts the
scent for opportunity. Its frequent companions are
selfishness, snobbery, and indolence.

The prayer of the humble pierces the clouds.

When you think you stand, take heed lest you fall.

Who can number the sand of the sea,
and the drops of rain,
and the days of eternity?

The gilding of the key will not
make it open the door better.

Seek not out the things that are too
hard for you, neither search the things
that are above your strength.

When you pray, enter into your closet, and
when you have shut the door, pray to your Father
which is in secret; and your Father which sees
in secret shall reward you openly.

> What if the little rain should say,
>   'As small a drop as I
> Can never refresh a drooping earth,
>   I'll tarry in the sky.'

The beginning of pride is when one departs from God,
and his heart is turned away from his Maker.

Who has deceived you so often as yourself?

Meekness is not weakness.

Meekness is surrendering to God.

Nothing will make us so charitable and tender to the
faults of others as to thoroughly examine ourselves.

Pride goes before destruction,
and a haughty spirit before a fall.

It is of no advantage for man to know much
unless he lives according to what he knows.

Talk to a man about himself,
and he will listen for hours.

Snobs talk as if they had begotten their ancestors.

> If the whole world followed you,
>   Followed to the letter,
> Tell me—if it followed you,
>   Would the world be better?

Exalt not yourself lest you fall.

Faith and meekness are a delight to God.

Humble yourselves, therefore, under the mighty hand
of God, that He may exalt you in due time.

People put a low estimate on the man who puts
too high an estimate on himself.

You can always spot a well-informed man—
his views are the same as yours.

Who can understand his errors?
Cleanse Thou me from secret faults.

If you were to list the ten smartest people,
who would be the other nine?

God speaks to man when man admits he has
absolutely nothing to say.

Before honor is humility.

Walk worthy of the vocation wherewith you are
called, with all lowliness and meekness, with
long suffering, forbearing one another in love,
endeavoring to keep the unity of the Spirit
in the bond of peace.

There is more hope of a fool than of a man
wise in his own conceit.

Seek not to be better than our neighbors
but better than ourselves.

He tried to be somebody
by trying to be like everybody,
which makes him a nobody.

If the best man's faults were written on his
forehead, he would draw his hat over his eyes.

Some men never feel small,
but these are the few men who are.

Better to speak wisdom foolishly
than to speak folly wisely.

A child can ask many questions
the wisest man cannot answer.

We may be taught by every person we meet.

Seeing ourselves as others see us wouldn't
do much good—we wouldn't believe it anyway.

Man shall ever stand in need of man.

Who is like unto the Lord our God,
Who dwells on high, Who humbles Himself
to behold the things that are in heaven,
and in the earth.

If my people, which are called by My name,
shall humble themselves, and pray, and seek My face,
and turn from their wicked ways; then will I hear
from heaven, and will forgive their sin,
and will heal their land.

Humility is that low sweet root,
from which all heavenly virtues shoot.

Receive with meekness the engrafted Word,
which is able to save your souls.

The wisdom of this world is foolishness with God.

Do the truth you know, and you shall learn
the truth you need to know.

If you have knowledge let others
light their candles by it.

He that swells in prosperity
will be sure to shrink in poverty.

Blessed are the meek, for they shall
inherit the earth.

Temperance

No man is free who cannot command himself.

Fine eloquence consists in saying all that should be,
not all that could be said.

> I always think before I speak.
> I find this rather balking,
> For by the time my thinking's done,
> Somebody else is talking.

Think all you speak, but speak not all you think.

Let your speech be short, comprehending much
in few words; be as one that knows
and yet holds his tongue.

Brevity is the soul of wit and even wit is a burden
when it talks too long.

A wholesome tongue is a tree of life.

A good listener is not only popular everywhere,
but after a while he knows something.

There is more hope for a fool than for a man
that is hasty with his words.

Silence is one of the great arts of conversation.

Set a watch, O Lord, before my mouth;
keep the door of my lips.

Nothing is opened more by mistake than the mouth.

In the multitude of words there wants not sin;
but he that refrains his lips is wise.

If any man offend not in word, the same is a
perfect man and able also to bridle the whole body.

Every idle word that men shall speak, they
shall give account thereof in the day of judgment.

Let no corrupt communication proceed
out of your mouth; but that which is good to
the use of edifying.

Death and life are in the power of the tongue.

Habit is either the best of servants
or the worst of masters.

Sow an act and you reap a habit.
Sow a habit and you reap a character.
Sow a character and you reap a destiny.

We first make our habits, and then our habits make us.

Habits are at first cobwebs, then cables.

Even a fool, when he holds his peace,
is counted wise: and he that shuts his lips
is esteemed a man of understanding.

They think too little who talk too much.

The chains of habit are generally too small
to be felt until they are too strong to be broken.

Habit, if not resisted, soon becomes necessity.

It is the neglect of timely repair
that makes rebuilding necessary.

We perform many acts automatically. We have
formed the habit of walking, eating, etc., without
conscious thought. In the moral realm, we can so
form the habit of living up to our better selves
that this also becomes automatic.

When a man has not a good reason for doing a thing,
he has one good reason for letting it alone.

Be sober, be vigilant; because your adversary
the devil, as a roaring lion, walks about,
seeking whom he may devour.

Being overly careful about tiny details
of one virtue can't make up for complete
neglect of another duty.

Moderation in temper is a virtue.
Moderation in principle is a vice.

A tree will not only lie as it falls,
but it will fall as it leans.

Lord, so teach us to number our days that we may
apply our hearts unto wisdom.

No gain is so certain as that which proceeds
from the economical use of what you already have.

If you know how to spend less than you get,
you have the philosopher's stone.

Prosperity's right hand is industry,
and her left hand is frugality.

Some people wait to start saving for a rainy day
until it starts sprinkling.

Thrift is a wonderful thing—and who doesn't
wish his ancestors had practiced it more?

A man is rich in proportion to the number of things
which he can afford to let alone.

The safest way to double your money is to
fold it over once and put it in your pocket.

Economy is in itself a source of great revenue.

The saving of money usually means
the saving of man. It means cutting off
indulgences or avoiding vicious habits.

Money is a good servant, but a poor master.

A penny saved is as good as a penny earned.

Riches are not an end of life,
but an instrument of life.

He is rich whose income is more than his expenses;
he is poor whose expenses exceed his income.

What does that man want who has enough?

Leisure for men of business and business for
men of leisure would cure many complaints.

We always have time enough if we but use it aright.

Good luck is a lazy man's estimate
of a worker's success.

He is already poverty-stricken whose
habits are not thrifty.

Gold has been the ruin of many.

Waste not, want not.

Willful waste makes woeful want.

The man who does nothing but wait for his
ship to come in has already missed the boat.

Luck is a very good word if you put a P before it.

Can a man take fire in his bosom, and his clothes
not be burned? Can one go upon hot coals,
and his feet not be burned?

Hard work is an accumulation of easy things
you didn't do when you should have.

Make your recreation servant to your business,
lest you become a servant to your recreation.

Waste of time is the most extravagant
and costly of all expenses.

Leisure is a beautiful garment,
but it will not do for constant wear.

'The longest way 'round is the shortest way home.'
'Make haste slowly.' 'Haste makes waste.' These are
all homely proverbs with the same meaning; namely,
careful painstaking effort pays in the long run.

When angry count ten before you speak;
if very angry, count a hundred.

Anger, if not restrained, is frequently more
hurtful to us than the injury that provokes it.

Temper, if ungoverned, governs the whole man.

He who can suppress a moment's anger
may prevent a day of sorrow.

It is not what people eat, but what they digest,
that makes them strong. It is not what they gain,
but what they save, that makes them rich.
It is not what they read, but what they remember,
that makes them learn.

Regret is an appalling waste of energy;
you can't build on it;
it is only good for wallowing in.

Commit a sin twice, and it will seem no longer a sin.

There are times when nothing a man can say
is nearly so powerful as saying nothing.

A stitch in time saves nine.

A covetous man's eye is not satisfied
with his portion.

The key to a lot of troubles
is the one that fits the ignition.

Statistics prove folks who drive like crazy are.

He who feasts every day feasts no day.

It is never safe to consider individuals in groups,
classes, or races. To ascribe virtues or vices
to all the individuals of a group is as senseless
as it is unjust and inaccurate.

The ally of tolerance is knowledge. As a rule,
understanding of another's nature
precludes hostility. This holds good between nations
and races as well as between individuals.

The excesses of our youth are drafts upon
our old age, payable, with interest,
about thirty years after date.

Folk who never do more than they get paid for
seldom get paid for more than they do.

Some live without working
and others work without living.

He is not poor who has little,
but he that desires much.

The first step in making a dream come true
is to wake up.

Thrift is essential to well-ordered living.

Wealth is a means to an end and not the end itself.

He who has little and wants less
is richer than he who has much and wants more.

A spender's solvency depends more upon his attitude
than upon his income.

He is richest who is content with the least.

He that buys what he does not want
will soon want what he cannot buy.

Many would never know want
had they not first known waste.

Choose rather to want less than to have more.

Silence is not always golden—
sometimes it is just plain yellow.

There would not be so many open mouths
if there were not so many open ears.

Discretion in speech is more than eloquence.

Gossip is putting 2 and 2 together and making 5.

How many friends would remain if all persons
knew what each said of the other?

A prudent wife is from the Lord.

Every wise woman builds her house:
but the foolish plucks it down with her hands.

*Herein are great rules of life contracted into
short sentences that may be easily impressed on
the memory and so recur habitually to the mind.*